For William

It Is Now

It is Now that
I lack. The very
motion of no motion.
The very comprehension of
nothing.

I am not, but I am very
Here.

I am lost, but I know how
I got here.

Show me the Way to
Nowhere, there
shall I unlearn Knowledge and
commit myself to Nothing but

the softest breath of air.

Now I Am Born

Now I am born.
Dark matterings of an obscene sort
drive me to realize that I am
incurably nerve-wracked.
Incorrigibly drawn to drive myself insane.

Lessons I have learned taught
me nothing,
Aphorisms void of
sense; meaning.

I cannot
learn, just
know and see
the stars feel
the breeze taste
the depth.

The particle of the moment is elusive. It drifts
between knowledge and the edge
of nonsense.

It betrays itself in simplicity; hides within me.

Sunrise Songs

Molasses voices blow through the dunes singing silent songs sipping harmony from seashells.

The gentle caresses of cyclical waves against the shore call to us as we lay side by side within our dusty dwelling.

A beam of light sneaks through cracks in the blinders, finding my eye. I follow its course to the window; peaking between plastic barriers and behold a brilliant sight.

An expansive sky lies above and beyond sand and infinite sea. Terraced cloudy fortresses catch blues and purples as light streams across the openness in 1000 colors.

I must catch myself before I get lost in the dazzling display.

"I am just me, I am just here" I whisper to myself as my wide eyes glisten with tears of wonder.

"This is a new day, this is a new time." A response resounds. "You are just here, you are just now. Exactly!"

I walk over to the bed, plant a kiss on your head. Time to make coffee.

The Conversation

on and on about the lost stories of lives:
experiences had in bars, little corner stores.

times had in big, bright cities... wondrous and foreign.
blissful country towns, strangers known as neighbors.

generous exploits, peaceful adversity, attainment of wholeness
through self-division and self-destruction.

we are the stories we write, the subjects of novella and
poem, protagonists in a neverending dream.

he goes on about philosophy and metaphysics:
huge secrets to be revealed, large spirits in tiny holes.

i yawn, as hours catch up. coffee sip, and on we go to politics:
corrupt losers, noble statesmen, fearless generals. i know no
better as he drawls on and on and my eyes wander and
thoughts too.

i daydream about taking myself on a journey or quest... travel
far
and wide to search out myself in the corners of the world.
might i be hiding in those little stores, bright cities, peaceful
villages?

SNAP to attention at the realization of being questioned...
making apologies with yet another sip of coffee and igniting a
deadly cylinder of necessity.

an argument ensues about the nature of things and our hands
begin to fly.

annoyed looks received for wild gesticulations and claims

unfounded.

tip drops on counter
cups stacked
plates removed.

i take my leave of chaotic subjects to enter the "orderly" world
of public transportation as the sun blinds me and the
brightness of this city sinks into my bones.

Sitting On The Trash Can

Sunchild came to me..
in Winters' cold death he sang
my soul's very depth.

Moondaughter upon
the nape of my neck she marks
a cool, icy, soft breath.

motor whining high,
drip drop from the canopy
melting snow glistens.

in the flash of the
Moment, the way you tell me
it does not matter.

dive deep within you.
it tells me the name of Now:
oil-smell, frost-drop... sit.

Rest.

Thawing

Wearied limbs rest now
Soaked through to the bone, deeply
Warm, soggy embrace

Deep marrow, freezing
Numb-boned apathy within
Frosty countenance

Sockets rush in deep caverns
Beginning with the process of internal erosion
Silencing various hums and inner processes

Sprouting

Subtle; flowing
an ongoing question mark
asking you... what?

What do you want?
Where are you going?

I can provide, but only up to a point.
I can carry you all the way, but you
need to take the first step.

Ageless, living
a vision of perspective
showing you... what?

A vast field on a high hill
overlooking a sea, by the forest.

The grass can tickle your ear
The high wind can lift you away.
The ocean shows you infinity,
The forest will pluck eternity for you
in every moment... the abundant fruit
is open
to YOUR call.

Bodhi Monastery

There are steel birds
flying through iron bars on their way
through the mists that I embrace.

A crow calls me amidst more flowery
sounds.

Rustlings and frantic breaths
Melt into larks and
sweet(ness) flowing into
a still, open sky.

Golden light
atop the highest drift
of clouds swaying liberated
over bright, green hills.

harmonica blues-
pigeons peck
at crumbs

It Is Now 2

spiralling scratchy voices
yearn to be smooth
deeply feeling melancholy
bittersweet heartfulness
jealous admiration for
assuming the greatness
that was mine (but small)

it is now, this achey blessing
a wide open door to comprehending
why sinking dialogues hit rock bottom

reaching out to accomplish greater things
finding no inspiration, reaching all the same

if i reach for now, then
it's then not now
the unfortunate reality
of the present

presently, sitting in front of flat screens
i test the waters of the inner sea
wondering if, perhaps, i'm free?

it is now, this wrenching confusion
a portal to bliss
a gateway beyond coping
with lost dreams
and frozen ones

diving into cold water

a shocking event
zippy floaters visioning
my back bare on the grass
staring at whisps of skysnow
puffed and fluffy

if i reach for the now to be
it won't be the way it would
if i hadn't reached for it now

scratchy voices fade off
testing those perilous waters
deeper than i can dive
i sink to float
fall to rise
rise
rise

emerge.

How Are You?

how am i?
good i guess
but what does that mean?

or is it just arrangements of words
we feed to each other
so we can keep on talking?

because if we do
we stumble across something
a bridge perhaps
which is just love
by a more tentative name.

rain falls softly-
traffic
whizzes by

Some Roof Somewhere

I am at this moment
whole, solid, completely
something to

connect the dots to (reveal)

it's hidden this
elusive balance this
unfortunate
reality

it
grows until the
girth and weight and length of the...
until it's too much.

i saw you walking down a deserted stretch of pavement
crumbling but crawling on despite the
grass in the cracks widening the
space (between) in between

like an expanding galax(ies) of thought i
am no longer
just floating, drifting

i just listen to these vague, distant chords
of acoustic rawness. voice scratchy but resonant,
foot tapping along to an imaginary beat.

it just fades into the wind and the "tip tap" of the
rain upon some roof

somewhere...

Leaving Work

mixing life and thought (explosive) i
wait for prophecies of ME to pan out

failure and crinkled leaves,
crunched into dust underfoot the
dwelling places of insecurities that have been
blown away...
...slowly fade into oblivion.

it slows, this grinding vibration...
electric appliances buzzing...
the power is cut, the rumble stilled.

windy slipstreams slide around cars,
waves of bass hit from some
broken hulk... cigarette smoke wafting

i sit, wait, wait...
and here it is... the-

Can't Sleep

crickets like dream-sounds
a sad, scrambling ache it
devours the inside of me
bright, burning uncertainty
like taking an eraser to the chalkboard
of mind.

the substance squiggles
it shows me itself bent forwards over
a stone while it flows through me

head like a black hole everything
disappears.

?

A vicious cycle
sitting out back smoking Spirits
nightsounds closing in like
comforting symphonies.

Miles from nowhere
mind a nomadic drifter
from dreams to judgement,
from pain to exhilaration.

Out on the still water
picturesque islands... devoid of dwellers.
only the gulls laying in wait to
snag a clam, catch a straggling fish
stuck in the tide like the
rest of us.

sky stretched out across
the span with frizzled cotton
clouds unraveling from within.

From Up To Down

It is a fresh perspective looking
from up to down watching millions of
ants in their city, serving their
queen. Watching grasshopper yogis
floating on their blades, waiting
for extraordinary things to take
place. Crickets in dark places
waiting for darkness to fall when
they sing the stories of the world.

Morning Light

sunlight pours through windows
expanding awareness

performing is difficult; futile
i'm just a bleeding heart
flying away like humming birds
motoring their way through
veils and dimensions
threaded through
impossible depths

interdimensional chaos
a million sparks courting possibilities
inspired by laughing faces
and glistening eyes

i don't know how to say
that i am a fluorescent melody
multi-layered masks
peeling away into nothing

when you get to the center
you rest in contentment
not jittery
no drowsiness
just effervescent bliss

Days Pass By

Days pass by like minutes
yet an hour can be eternity.
A continuous flow of bass noises.
Those moments when I realize that
happening will stop.
Seconds tick by and I lose myself
in the midst of activity.
A crackling.
A man walks in this store
and for a split second
I'm not sure what to do.
Plastic cases hit counters.
I always say life is a gift.
But for me it is given by
itself to itself;
an entire world of mirrors.
A high rattling whine.
Wondering whether this processes
could be revamped
into something spectacular.
Images of cars pass by the windows.
And it fades away into deeper vibrations.

It Is Now 3

It is Now
that pulses
through me.
The sweetest nectar
of essence.
It always has been,
is,
always will be:
a photon flying
into my retina
until no light comes.

out of the
blackest mucky swamp-
a white lotus

Advice From Bashō

Keep it simple.
Be a frog
sitting on a lily pad.
Catch a fly.
Splash the water
as you jump in
a drop flies into
the air.
Ripples on the
surface
extend and
they find the shape
of the waters'
edge.

Remember When

Remember when stars glittered and
the yawning blackness of the sky
was pierced with infinite points
of light so far behind Now that they
showed themselves to you even
though they might have died and the
moon had almost reached her apex
and you looked at her and smiled?

One Mind, One Thought

One mind, one thought
at a time. The past is
gone as soon as it is
the present: becomes the
future. One heart. It
is shared by billions.
We walk along smugly
thinking that only we
know. I live inside
echoes reverberating
through my dreams.
Yesterday I found a
quarter on the subway
covered in dust only a
few shiny glints to
distinguish it. I got
stuck wondering what
hand dropped it.

We Are Stronger

we are stronger
than our bones
brave enough to
face nightmares.
we hold keys to
our own lives.

Mastery

tranquility reigns and I
am the master of thoughts.
within my heart there are
light years-wide plains where
you are welcome to take
shelter, we are the
progeny of titans.

Aspire

shimmering lakes mirror-like
calm with the limitless depth
of miles.
I float on a raft
made of aspiration
that is powered in
movement by mind.
carving arches in
the richness of the
air, silver fish of
delight jump higher
than my spirits,
rope your dreams to clouds
pull yourself along with the Sun's
vast light.

To Whom Life May Concern:

I am at the fount of myself,
the present moment.
Outwardly tethered,
within I'm freer
than a balloon
floating through open sky.

Words take shape
in the gateway,
but behind it
there are mere tones
a swath of probabilities
unleashed by ink
paper and
my own wrist.

I have broken trysts
injured innocence and
I'm sorry for the
tearing of promises from
unexpecting hands.

To be born we must
be unborn first.

So as not to leave
a legacy of tears
I will ignite the
blossoming of every
being I can manage
to rouse from

their troubled slumber.

Thank you for this opportunity,
Robin Stuart-Tilley

www.ingramcontent.com/pod-product-compliance
Lightning Source LLC
Chambersburg PA
CBHW071804020426

42331CB00008B/2405